contents

oatmeal chocolate chip cookies

MAKES ABOUT 4 DOZEN

These cookies contain wheat germ, which can go rancid quickly; always keep it refrigerated.

- 1 cup light-brown sugar, packed
- 1 cup granulated sugar
- 1 cup (2 sticks) unsalted butter, room temperature
- 2 large eggs, room temperature
- 1 teaspoon pure vanilla extract
- 3 cups rolled oats
- 1 cup plus 2 tablespoons all-purpose flour
- 1 teaspoon baking soda
- 1 teaspoon baking powder
- ½ cup wheat germ
- 6 ounces semisweet chocolate chips
- 1 cup raisins
- 1 cup shelled walnuts, coarsely chopped

1. Preheat the oven to 350°F. In the bowl of an electric mixer fitted with the paddle attachment, combine brown sugar, granulated sugar, and butter. Starting on low speed and increasing to medium, beat until mixture is creamy and fluffy, about 5 minutes. Add eggs and vanilla, scrape down sides of the bowl with a rubber spatula, and mix to combine.

2. Combine oats, flour, baking soda, baking powder, and wheat germ in a large bowl; stir to combine. Add to butter mixture; mix on low speed just to combine, 10 to 15 seconds. Remove from mixer; stir in chocolate chips, raisins, and walnuts.

3. Line baking sheets with parchment paper. With damp hands, shape 2 tablespoons of dough into a ball; place on a baking sheet. Repeat, spacing cookies 2 inches apart. Bake until golden brown, 15 to 17 minutes, rotating baking sheets between oven shelves halfway through baking time. Transfer to wire racks to cool.

torie's chocolate-chunk toffee cookies

MAKES ABOUT 2 ½ DOZEN

Torie Hallock makes these delicious cookies at Martha's house in Maine. Toffee pieces can be found in the baking section of grocery stores.

- 1½ cups all-purpose flour
- 1 teaspoon baking soda
- 1 cup (2 sticks) unsalted butter, room temperature
- ¾ cup packed light-brown sugar
- ¾ cup granulated sugar
- 1 large egg
- 1 teaspoon pure vanilla extract
- 1½ cup oats
- 1 cup dried cherries
- 4½ ounces bittersweet chocolate, coarsely chopped
- 1 cup toffee pieces

1. Preheat the oven to 350°F. Line two baking sheets with parchment paper; set aside. In a large bowl, sift together flour and baking soda.

2. In the bowl on an electric mixer fitted with the paddle attachment, cream butter and both sugars on medium-high speed until light and fluffy, 2 to 3 minutes, scraping down sides of the bowl once or twice during mixing. Add egg, mix on high speed to combine. Add vanilla; mix to combine. Scrape down the sides of the bowl.

3. Working in additions, add flour mixture to egg mixture on low speed until well combined. Add oats, cherries, chocolate, and toffee pieces; mix to combine.

4. Spoon a heaping tablespoon of dough onto a baking sheet. Repeat, spacing 2 inches apart.

5. Bake cookies until golden brown, about 10 minutes. Transfer to a wire rack to cool. Store in an airtight container up to 2 days.

big ginger cookies

MAKES ABOUT 1 DOZEN

Sanding sugar is coarser than granulated sugar and adds sparkle to finished baked goods.

- 2½ cups all-purpose flour
- 2¼ teaspoons baking soda
- ½ teaspoon salt
- 1 tablespoon ground ginger
- ½ teaspoon ground allspice
- ½ teaspoon ground white pepper
- 1 cup (2 sticks) plus 2 tablespoons unsalted butter
- ½ cup packed light-brown sugar
- 6 tablespoons unsulfured molasses
- 1 large egg
- ½ cup sanding or granulated sugar

1. Preheat the oven to 350°F. Line two baking sheets with parchment paper, and set aside. In a medium bowl, whisk flour, baking soda, salt, ginger, allspice, and white pepper; set aside.

2. In the bowl of an electric mixer fitted with the paddle attachment, combine butter with light-brown and granlated sugars until light and fluffy. Beat in the molasses and egg; mix well. Add remaining dry ingredients, and beat just until combined. Form dough into a ball, and cover with plastic wrap; refrigerate until firm, at least 2 hours or overnight.

3. Remove dough from refrigerator. Using an ice-cream scoop, shape dough into 2-inch-diameter balls. Pour sanding sugar into a large bowl, and roll balls in the sanding sugar, coating well. Place cookies on prepared baking sheets, spaced 4 inches apart; flatten each into a 3-inch-diameter disk.

4. Transfer cookies to oven and bake until brown, 12 to 15 minutes. Remove from oven, and transfer to a wire rack to cool. Store in an airtight container for up to 2 days.

milk-chocolate chunk cookies

MAKES ABOUT 1 DOZEN

You can substitute semisweet chocolate chunks or chips for the milk chocolate.

- 2 cups all-purpose flour
- ½ teaspoon baking soda
- 1 teaspoon salt
- 1 cup (2 sticks) unsalted butter, room temperature
- 1 teaspoon pure vanilla extract
- ¾ cup packed dark-brown sugar
- ½ cup granulated sugar
- 1 large egg
- 10 ounces milk chocolate, cut into ½-inch chunks (2 cups)

1. Preheat the oven to 375°F. Line two baking sheets with parchment paper, and set aside. In a medium bowl, whisk together flour, baking soda, and salt; set aside.

2. In the bowl of an electric mixer fitted with the paddle attachment, combine butter and vanilla; beat until fluffy. Add both sugars, and beat until light. Add egg, and beat until combined. Add reserved dry ingredients; beat on low speed just until combined. Stir in chocolate chunks. Form dough into a ball, and cover with plastic wrap; refrigerate until firm, at least 2 hours or overnight.

3. Remove dough from refrigerator. Using an ice-cream scoop, shape dough into 2-inch-diameter balls. Place balls on prepared baking sheets, spaced 4 inches apart. Flatten each ball into a 3-inch-diameter disk. Chill until firm.

4. Transfer to oven, and bake until edges are golden but centers are still soft, 15 to 17 minutes. Remove from oven. Transfer to a wire rack to cool completely. Store in an airtight container up to 2 days.

peach-oatmeal cookies

MAKES ABOUT 3 DOZEN

If you want these cookies crisp, leave them out overnight uncovered; for moist cookies, wrap them well once they've cooled.

- 3 large peaches, or 1¼ pounds frozen peaches, thawed and drained
- 1 tablespoon fresh lemon juice
- 3 tablespoons unsalted butter, room temperature
- ½ cup dark-brown sugar, packed
- 6 tablespoons granulated sugar
- 1 large egg
- 1 tablespoon pure vanilla extract
- 1½ cups plus 1 tablespoon rolled oats
- 1¼ cups all-purpose flour
- 1 teaspoon baking soda
- ½ teaspoon cinnamon
- ½ teaspoon salt
- ¾ cup sun-dried cherries, chopped

1. Preheat the oven to 350°F. Line two baking sheets with parchment paper. Pit, peel, and dice two of the peaches. (If using frozen peaches, set aside ¾ cup.) Place diced peaches in a saucepan; add lemon juice. Cook over medium-low heat, stirring, until peaches are broken down, about 20 minutes. Using a whisk, mash peaches; let cool.

2. Meanwhile, dice remaining peach or reserved frozen peaches.

3. In the bowl of an electric mixer fitted with the paddle attachment, beat butter and sugars on high until well combined, about 2 minutes. Add egg and vanilla; beat until combined. Beat in mashed peaches. Add diced peaches; stir in by hand.

4. In a bowl, mix oats, flour, baking soda, cinnamon, salt, and cherries. Stir into peach mixture by hand until well combined. Drop a heaping tablespoonful onto a prepared sheet; dampen finger and gently flatten. Repeat, spacing 2 inches apart.

5. Bake until very golden brown and crisp around the edges, 20 to 25 minutes. Transfer to wire racks to cool.

oatmeal fruit cookies

MAKES ABOUT 4 DOZEN

This is the best-ever version of the traditional oatmeal-raisin cookie: chewy, spicy, and filled with fruit.

- 4 tablespoons (½ stick) unsalted butter
- 1 cup firmly packed dark brown sugar
- ½ cup granulated sugar
- 1 large egg
- ⅔ cup milk
- 1 teaspoon vanilla extract
- 1½ cups sifted all-purpose flour
- 1 teaspoon baking soda
- 1 teaspoon cinnamon
- ¼ teaspoon ground cloves
- ¼ teaspoon ground nutmeg
- 3 cups rolled oats
- 1 cup dried fruit such as figs, apples, and apricots
- 1 cup raisins

1. In the bowl of an electric mixer fitted with the paddle attachment, cream together butter, sugars, egg, milk, and vanilla.

2. In a large bowl, sift together flour, baking soda, and spices; and add to butter mixture.

3. Stir in oats, mixing well. Stir in dried fruit and raisins. Place the dough in the refrigerator to chill, for several hours.

4. Preheat the oven to 350°F. Drop batter by teaspoonfuls, about 2 inches apart, onto parchment-lined baking sheets. Bake for 12 minutes; transfer to wire racks to cool.

oatmeal-pecan chocolate chunk cookies

MAKES ABOUT 2 DOZEN

You can buy chocolate that has already been chunked, or simply cut up your favorite chocolate.

- 2 cups all-purpose flour
- ½ teaspoon salt
- 1 teaspoon baking powder
- 1 teaspoon baking soda
- 1 cup (2 sticks) unsalted butter, room temperature
- 1 cup packed light-brown sugar
- 1 cup granulated sugar
- 1 tablespoon pure vanilla extract
- 3 tablespoons milk
- 2 large eggs
- 3 cups old-fashioned oats
- 12 ounces semisweet chocolate, chopped into ½-inch chunks
- 1⅓ cups (5 ounces) coarsely chopped pecans

1. In a medium bowl, whisk together flour, salt, baking powder, and baking soda. Set dry ingredients aside.

2. In the bowl of an electric mixer fitted with the paddle attachment, combine butter with both sugars; beat until light and fluffy. Add the vanilla, milk, and eggs; mix well. Add the reserved dry ingredients, and beat until just combined. Remove bowl from mixer, and fold in oats, chocolate, and pecans. Place dough in the refrigerator until firm, at least 2 hours or overnight.

3. Preheat the oven to 350°F. Line two baking sheets with parchment paper, and set aside. Remove dough from refrigerator. Using an ice-cream scoop, shape into 2-inch-diameter balls. Place 6 balls on each baking sheet, spaced 4 inches apart, and press down to flatten balls into 3-inch-diameter disks.

4. Transfer to oven. Bake until golden, but still soft in center, 15 to 16 minutes. Transfer to a wire rack to cool completely. Repeat with remaining dough. Store in an airtight container up to 2 days.

ne plus ultra cookies

MAKES ABOUT 1 DOZEN

Webster's Dictionary defines "ne plus ultra" as "the peak of achievement." These cookies begin as traditional chocolate chip, and are enhanced with raisins and pecans.

- 8 tablespoons (1 stick) unsalted butter
- 2/3 cup firmly packed dark brown sugar
- 1/4 cup granulated sugar
- 1 teaspoon vanilla extract
- 2 large eggs
- 1 1/4 cups sifted all-purpose flour
- 1/2 teaspoon salt
- 1/2 teaspoon baking soda
- 1 cup semisweet chocolate chips
- 1 cup raisins
- 1 cup pecans, finely chopped

1. Preheat the oven to 350°F. Line a baking sheet with parchment paper; set aside.

2. In the bowl of an electric mixer fitted with the paddle attachment, cream butter and sugars until fluffy. Add vanilla and eggs; beat well. Sift together flour, salt, and baking soda; add to butter mixture. Beat again. Stir in chocolate chips, raisins, and pecans.

3. Form dough into 2 1/2-inch balls. Place on prepared baking sheet, and press to 1 inch thick with palm of hand.

4. Bake for 20 minutes, or until golden. Transfer to wire racks to cool.

mocha almond cookies

MAKES ABOUT 2 DOZEN

Dark chocolate dough is rolled in sugar; as it bakes, the sugar will "crackle," exposing the bittersweet cookie within.

- 4 ounces unsweetened chocolate
- 8 tablespoons (1 stick) unsalted butter
- 6 tablespoons coffee-flavored liqueur
- 2 large eggs
- ¾ cup granulated sugar, plus more for rolling
- 1⅓ cups sifted all-purpose flour
- ¾ teaspoon baking powder
- 1 cup blanched almonds, finely ground
- Sifted confectioners' sugar, for rolling

1. In a pan, melt chocolate and butter over low heat. Stir in coffee liqueur; keep mixture warm. In the bowl of an electric mixer fitted with the paddle attachment, beat together eggs and sugar until fluffy. Stir flavored chocolate into egg mixture. Sift together flour and baking powder; stir into chocolate-and-egg mixture, and beat well. Stir in ground almonds.

2. Transfer to the refrigerator, and chill dough until firm. Form dough into 1-inch balls and chill again for 10 minutes.

3. Preheat the oven to 325°F. Remove balls from refrigerator, and roll first in granulated sugar and then in confectioners' sugar, coating well. Place on baking sheets.

4. Transfer to oven, and bake for 15 minutes. Transfer to wire racks to cool.

coconut cream sandwiches

MAKES ABOUT 3 DOZEN

- 1¼ cups whole unblanched almonds (7 ounces)
- 1 cup superfine sugar
- 2 large egg whites
- 1¼ teaspoons pure almond extract
- 1½ cups heavy cream
- 1¼ cups shredded sweetened coconut

1. Preheat the oven to 350°F. Process almonds and 2 tablespoons sugar in a food processor to a fine powder, about 1 minute. Transfer to the bowl of an electric mixer fitted with the paddle attachment. Add remaining sugar, egg whites, and 1 teaspoon almond extract; mix on medium-low speed to combine.

2. Drop rounded teaspoonfuls of dough on a parchment-lined baking sheet, 1 to 2 inches apart. Bake until very light brown, 15 to 17 minutes. Place sheet on a wire rack. Let cookies cool on sheet for 15 minutes before transferring to racks to cool completely.

3. Meanwhile, pour cream and remaining ¼ teaspoon almond extract into a chilled metal bowl and whip until soft peaks form. Turn half the cookies over, so that the bottoms are facing up. Place a heaping teaspoon of whipped cream on the underside of each cookie and sprinkle with coconut. Place a second cookie on top of each filled half to form a sandwich. Serve immediately or refrigerate for up to 2 hours until ready to serve.

pecan butter cookies with chocolate chunks

MAKES 2 DOZEN

If you prefer a chewy cookie, bake for fifteen minutes. For cakier cookies, bake for the full twenty minutes.

- 11 ounces (about 2 ½ cups) pecan halves
- ¼ cup plus 2 tablespoons vegetable oil
- ¾ teaspoon salt
- 1 cup (2 sticks) unsalted butter, room temperature
- 1 cup packed light-brown sugar
- 2 large eggs, well beaten
- 2 teaspoons pure vanilla extract
- 3½ cups all-purpose flour
- 2 teaspoons baking soda
- 10 ounces bittersweet chocolate, chopped into chunks

1. Set aside 3 ounces (about 48) pecan halves. Combine remaining 8 ounces pecans, vegetable oil, and ½ teaspoon salt in the jar of a food processor. Process until mixture is very smooth and creamy, scraping down the sides if needed. Set pecan butter aside.

2. In the bowl of an electric mixer fitted with the paddle attachment, cream butter and sugar on medium-high speed until light and fluffy, about 2 minutes. Scrape down sides of bowl with a rubber spatula. Add eggs, a little at a time, beating to combine between each addition. Add vanilla, and beat to combine. Add pecan butter, and beat to combine, scraping sides as needed with a rubber spatula.

3. Sift together flour, baking soda, and remaining ¼ teaspoon salt. With the mixer on low, add flour mixture in several additions. Use a rubber spatula to scrape sides as needed. Stir in chocolate chunks. Wrap dough in plastic, and chill at least 1 hour.

4. Preheat the oven to 350°F. Line two baking sheets with parchment paper; set aside.

5. Form the dough into twenty-four 1½-inch balls. Press two pecan halves into each ball, and place balls about 2 inches apart on prepared baking sheets. Bake until cookies are golden around the edges and just set, 15 to 20 minutes. Remove from oven; let stand several minutes before transferring to wire racks to cool completely.

fruit jumbles

MAKES 2 1/2 DOZEN

The pecans may be replaced with other nuts or an additional cup of granola.

- 1 cup unsalted pecans, coarsely chopped
- 2 cups dried fruits, such as pineapple, apricots, cranberries, and golden raisins
- 1 1/2 cups granola cereal
- 1/2 teaspoon salt
- 2/3 cup light corn syrup
- 2 tablespoons unsalted butter
- 1 tablespoon orange juice
- 1 teaspoon grated orange zest

1. Preheat the oven to 350°F. Spread the chopped pecans on a rimmed baking sheet. Bake until fragrant, about 10 minutes. Transfer pecans to a bowl to cool.

2. Cut the dried fruit, except raisins, into 1/4-inch pieces. In a medium bowl, combine all of the dried fruit, pecans, granola, and salt; set aside.

3. In a small saucepan, combine corn syrup, butter, and orange juice. Set the pan over medium heat until the butter has melted, about 4 minutes. Remove from heat, and stir in the orange zest.

4. Pour corn-syrup mixture over fruit mixture; stir well. Set aside until completely cool, about 1 hour.

5. Using a 1 1/4-inch ice-cream scoop or a tablespoon, form cooled mixture into 30 balls. Place into paper mini-muffin cups or in a single layer in an airtight container, and refrigerate until cold, about 30 minutes. Store in an airtight container, refrigerated, up to 1 week.

butter cream cookies with chocolate glaze

MAKES ABOUT 3 DOZEN

This rich cookie with its delicious chocolate glaze is based on a traditional French recipe.

- 12 tablespoons (1½ sticks) unsalted butter
- ¾ cup sifted confectioners' sugar
- 1 large egg
- 1½ cups sifted all-purpose flour
- ½ teaspoon salt
- Chocolate Glaze (recipe below)

1. In the bowl of an electric mixer fitted with the paddle attachment, cream butter. Add confectioners' sugar and beat until smooth. Stir in egg. Sift together flour and salt; add to butter mixture, and beat well. Transfer dough to the refrigerator, and chill dough until firm.

2. Preheat the oven to 350°F. Roll out the dough to a ⅛ inch thickness; cut into shapes. Bake for 12 minutes. Remove from oven, and transfer to wire racks to cool.

chocolate glaze

- 6 ounces semisweet chocolate

Melt chocolate slowly over low heat. Dip cookies into warm melted chocolate and allow to set.

coconut almond cookies

MAKES ABOUT 3 DOZEN

These cookies have a complex, nutty flavor.

- 1 cup finely shredded coconut
- 1 cup (2 sticks) unsalted butter
- ¼ teaspoon salt
- ½ cup sifted confectioners' sugar
- 1 teaspoon pure almond extract
- 2¼ cups sifted cake flour
- ¾ cup blanched almonds, finely ground
- Almond Butter Cream Icing (recipe below)

1. Preheat the oven to 325°F. Spread shredded coconut in a thin layer on a baking sheet; transfer to oven and toast until light golden brown, about 20 minutes. Stir occasionally.

2. In the bowl of an electric mixer fitted with the paddle attachment, cream butter with the salt. Gradually add sugar, beating until fluffy. Add almond extract and toasted coconut. Add flour, a little at a time. Stir in almonds. Transfer to refrigerator, and chill dough for several hours.

3. Preheat the oven to 325°F. Roll out the dough to a ¼ inch thickness and cut into desired shapes. Transfer to the oven and bake for 18 to 20 minutes. Transfer to wire racks to cool and ice with almond butter cream icing.

almond butter cream icing

- ½ cup (1 stick) unsalted butter
- 1 cup sifted confectioners' sugar
- ¼ teaspoon salt
- 1 teaspoon pure almond extract
- 1 cup toasted coconut

In the bowl of an electric mixer fitted with the paddle attachment, cream butter. Add sugar and salt, and beat until fluffy. Stir in almond extract. Spread on cookies and top with coconut.

key-lime sablés

MAKES 2 DOZEN

Use square cookie cutters to prepare these cookies; bake the cut-out windows for extra nibbles.

- 1⅓ cups flour, plus more for work surface
- ⅓ cup confectioners' sugar, plus more for dusting
- 1½ tablespoons granulated sugar
- ¼ teaspoon coarse salt
- ¾ cup (1½ sticks) unsalted butter, chilled and cut into pieces
- 1½ teaspoons pure lime extract
- Key-Lime Curd (recipe follows)

1. Place flour, confectioners' sugar, granulated sugar, and salt in jar of a food processor. Pulse until well combined. Add butter; pulse until coarse crumbs form. Add lime extract; pulse to mix.
2. Transfer the dough to a clean work surface, and flatten, forming a disk. Wrap the dough in plastic, and transfer to refrigerator. Chill until very firm, at least 2 hours.
3. Preheat the oven to 325°F. Line a baking sheet with parchment paper; set aside.
4. On a lightly floured surface, roll out the dough to a ⅛-inch thickness. Using a 1¾-inch fluted cookie cutter, cut the dough into squares. Using a 1-inch fluted cutter, cut windows from half of the squares. Place squares on the prepared baking sheet, spaced about 1 inch apart.
5. Bake until just golden, 15 to 17 minutes. Transfer to a wire rack to cool completely.
6. To assemble the sandwiches, spread 1 teaspoon lime curd on the bottom of the full squares. Dust the cut out squares with confectioners' sugar; then place on top of the curd, forming little sandwiches. Refrigerate until firm, about 20 minutes.

key-lime curd

MAKES ¾ CUP

- ½ cup sugar
- 2 large eggs, lightly beaten
- ¼ cup freshly squeezed key-lime juice plus 2 teaspoons grated zest (6 limes)
- 4 tablespoons unsalted butter, cut into small pieces

1. Combine sugar, eggs, lime juice, and zest in a medium nonreactive saucepan. Set over medium-low heat; cook, whisking constantly, until mixture thickens and holds the mark of whisk, about 20 minutes.
2. Remove from heat; whisk in butter, a piece at a time, until well combined. Strain through a sieve into a glass bowl. Lay plastic wrap directly on surface to prevent a skin from forming. Chill 3 hours.

chocolate sugar cookies

MAKES ABOUT 3 DOZEN

To slightly reduce the number of calories in these cookies, coat just the edges with sugar.

- ⅔ cup packed light-brown sugar
- ⅓ cup plus 1½ tablespoons granulated sugar
- 4 tablespoons unsalted butter, cut into pieces
- 1 teaspoon pure vanilla extract
- 2 large egg whites
- ¾ cup Dutch cocoa powder, sifted
- ¾ cup all-purpose flour
- Pinch of salt

1. Preheat the oven to 350°F. In the bowl of an electric mixer fitted with the paddle attachment, combine brown sugar, ⅓ cup granulated sugar, butter, and vanilla, and mix on medium-high speed until well combined. Add egg whites, and mix until combined.

2. In a small bowl, whisk together cocoa, flour, and salt. Add to sugar-and-butter mixture, and mix on medium until flour is completely incorporated. Turn this mixture out onto a piece of parchment or wax paper, and roll into a 1¾-by-8½-inch log. Chill for at least 1 hour or overnight.

3. Remove paper, and slice log crosswise into ¼-inch-thick pieces. Place remaining 1½ tablespoons granulated sugar in a small bowl, and dip each piece of dough in sugar, coating all sides; transfer to parchment-lined baking sheet 1 inch apart. Bake about 14 minutes for chewy cookies; for crisp cookies, bake 2 to 3 minutes more. Transfer the paper with cookies onto a wire rack to cool completely.

chocolate coin cookies

MAKES ABOUT 3 DOZEN

For a beautiful presentation, wrap these cookies in metallic foils.

- 8 tablespoons (1 stick) unsalted butter, room temperature
- ½ cup plus 2 tablespoons packed light-brown sugar
- 1 large egg
- 1 cup unsweetened cocoa powder
- ½ cup plus 3 tablespoons all-purpose flour, plus more for work surface
- ½ teaspoon salt
- 1 teaspoon grated orange zest (optional)
- ¼ cup granulated sugar

1. In the bowl of an electric mixer fitted with the paddle attachment, cream butter and brown sugar until light and fluffy, about 3 minutes. Add egg; mix until well combined.

2. In a large bowl, whisk together cocoa powder, flour, salt, and orange zest, if using. Add flour mixture to egg mixture; continue mixing until the ingredients are just combined, scraping down sides of the bowl.

3. Scrape dough onto a piece of plastic wrap; flatten into a disk. Wrap, and chill at least 1 hour or overnight.

4. Preheat the oven to 350°F. Line two baking sheets with parchment paper. Place granulated sugar in a small bowl.

5. On a lightly floured work surface, roll out the dough to a ¼-inch thickness. Using a 2-inch-round cutter, cut out cookies. Carefully press each cookie into granulated sugar. Transfer cookies to sheets, spaced ½ inch apart.

6. Bake until cookies are firm, about 12 minutes. Transfer to a wire rack to cool. Wrap in foil. Store in an airtight container up to 1 week.

chocolate orange cookies

MAKES ABOUT 3 DOZEN

Chocolate and orange is one of those magical combinations that enhances both flavors without disguising either.

- 8 tablespoons (1 stick) unsalted butter
- ⅔ cup sugar
- 1 large egg
- Zest of 1 orange
- 1 tablespoon orange-flavored liqueur
- 1¾ cups sifted all-purpose flour
- 1 teaspoon baking powder
- Pinch of salt
- ½ cup grated semisweet chocolate

1. In the bowl of an electric mixer fitted with the paddle attachment, cream butter and sugar. Beat in egg, zest, and liqueur. Mix until smooth. Sift together flour, baking powder, and salt, and add slowly to butter mixture. Beat in chocolate. Transfer to refrigerator to chill dough for several hours.

2. Preheat the oven to 325°F. Roll out the dough to a ¼-inch thickness and cut into shapes. Bake until golden, about 15 minutes. Transfer to wire racks to cool.

bourbon currant cookies

MAKES ABOUT 6 DOZEN

These dense, rich cookies need no frosting or decoration, just a brush of egg glaze before baking.

- ½ pound (2 sticks) unsalted butter
- 1 cup sugar
- 1 large egg
- 3 cups sifted all-purpose flour
- ⅓ cup bourbon
- ½ cup dried currants
- 1 large egg lightly beaten
- 4 tablespoons heavy cream, for glaze

1. Preheat the oven to 350°F. In the bowl of an electric mixer fitted with the paddle attachment, cream together butter and sugar. Add egg, flour, bourbon, and currants; mix well.

2. Roll out the dough to a ¼-inch thickness and cut into desired shapes. Brush cookies with egg-glaze mixture.

3. Transfer to the oven, and bake for 12 to 15 minutes. Transfer to wire racks to cool.

espresso shortbread

MAKES ABOUT 2 DOZEN

A simple shortbread with a sophisticated coffee flavor.

- ½ pound (2 sticks) unsalted butter
- ½ cup firmly packed light-brown sugar
- 1 teaspoon pure vanilla extract
- ¾ teaspoon powdered instant coffee
- 2¼ cups sifted all-purpose flour
- ¼ teaspoon salt

1. In the bowl of an electric mixer fitted with the paddle attachment, cream butter and sugar until fluffy. Add vanilla and coffee. In a bowl, sift together flour and salt; add to butter mixture and beat well. Transfer dough to refrigerator and chill until firm.

2. Preheat the oven to 325°F. Roll out the dough to a ¼-inch thickness and cut into 2-inch-by-5-inch bars. Prick with a fork. Score middles of bars with a knife.

3. Bake until light golden brown, 20 to 25 minutes. Transfer to wire racks to cool.

german butter cookies

MAKES ABOUT 12 DOZEN

An old-fashioned cookie that can be rolled and cut and still has a nice, light texture after baking.

- 1 cup granulated sugar
- 1 cup sifted confectioners' sugar
- ½ pound (2 sticks) unsalted butter
- 1 cup vegetable oil
- 2 large eggs, lightly beaten
- 1 teaspoon pure vanilla extract
- 5½ cups sifted all-purpose flour
- 1 teaspoon cream of tartar
- 1 teaspoon baking soda
- Royal Icing (recipe below)
- Colored sugar

1. In the bowl of an electric mixer fitted with the paddle attachment, cream sugars and butter. Add oil; blend in eggs and vanilla. Beat well. Sift together flour, cream of tartar, and baking soda. Add to sugar mixture; beat again. Transfer dough to the refrigerator and chill at least 6 hours.

2. Preheat the oven to 350°F. Roll out the dough to a ¼-inch thickness and cut into shapes. Bake for 8 to 10 minutes. Transfer to wire racks to cool.

royal icing

- 1 cup confectioners' sugar
- 1 large egg white
- Food coloring

Mix together confectioners' sugar and egg white; divide among small bowls and tint each a different color. Spread or pipe onto cookies and allow to set.

jam sandwich cookies

MAKES ABOUT 4 DOZEN SANDWICHES

For best results, roll out the dough as thinly as possible.

- 8 tablespoons (1 stick) unsalted butter
- 1 cup sugar, plus more for sprinkling
- 1 large egg
- 2 scant tablespoons water
- 1 teaspoon vanilla extract
- 1 teaspoon cream of tartar
- ¼ teaspoon salt
- 2 ¼ cups all-purpose flour, plus more for work surface
- Strawberry or raspberry jam, melted

1. In the bowl of an electric mixer fitted with the paddle attachment, cream butter. Add sugar gradually, and beat until mixture is light-colored and fluffy. Beat in egg, water, and vanilla.

2. Sift together cream of tartar, salt, and flour, and stir into sugar-butter mixture. Wrap dough in plastic, and transfer to the refrigerator to chill for several hours.

3. Preheat the oven to 400°F. Flour a work surface. Divide dough into quarters; keep portions not being rolled out wrapped in refrigerator. With a floured rolling pin, roll out dough as thinly as possible. Cut into shapes. Spread one cookie with melted jam, and top with matching shape. Sprinkle top with sugar and place on a parchment-lined baking sheet. Repeat until all dough is used.

4. Bake until cookies are lightly browned, 5 to 7 minutes. Transfer to wire racks to cool.

almond lace cookies

MAKES ABOUT 3 DOZEN

These cookies can be left flat or rolled into cones or cylinders. They can also be dipped in chocolate.

- 4 tablespoons unsalted butter
- 2 tablespoons heavy cream
- 1 tablespoon orange liqueur
- ½ cup whole unblanched almonds, ground medium fine
- 1 tablespoon all-purpose flour
- ½ cup sugar

1. Preheat the oven to 375°F. Line a baking sheet with parchment paper. In a small saucepan over medium heat, combine butter, cream, and orange liqueur. When butter has melted, stir in remaining ingredients with a wooden spoon. Cook until gently bubbling, 2 to 3 minutes. Remove from heat and keep warm.

2. Place 5 half teaspoons of batter 1½ inches apart on prepared baking sheet (this is as many as you can mold while hot). Bake until lightly browned and crisp, 6 to 7 minutes.

3. Remove from the oven and let sit for 1 to 2 minutes. Working quickly, lay each cookie over a cone-shaped object (we used a water-cooler cup), pressing edges together. Alternatively, roll cookies around the handle of a wooden spoon, pressing the edges together to form a cylinder. Continue baking and forming the cookies until you've used all of the batter. Transfer to a wire rack to cool.

peanut butter no-bakes

MAKES ABOUT 3 ½ DOZEN

Creamy peanut butter works best in this recipe. If you prefer, the melted chocolate can be drizzled onto the cookies instead of piped.

- 1½ cups old-fashioned oatmeal
- 1 cup creamy peanut butter
- 1½ cups nonfat dry milk
- 4 tablespoons (½ stick) unsalted butter
- 2 tablespoons honey
- ½ cup (about 2 ounces) semisweet chocolate morsels

1. Preheat the oven to 350°F. Spread oatmeal in an ungreased baking pan, and toast until it is lightly browned, about 11 minutes, shaking once. Set aside to cool.

2. In a medium bowl, combine peanut butter and dry milk. Stir in toasted oatmeal, and set aside.

3. In a small saucepan over medium heat, melt butter. Stir in honey. Pour butter mixture over peanut-butter mixture, and stir until well combined. Allow to cool slightly.

4. Shape into about 40 logs, each about 2 ½ inches long. Place logs on a wire rack or a parchment-lined baking sheet, and set aside.

5. Place chocolate morsels in a small heat-proof bowl, set over a pan of gently simmering water. Stir occasionally until chocolate is melted, about 2 minutes. Remove from heat, and transfer the melted chocolate to a pastry bag fitted with a #3 plain round tip. Pipe chocolate onto cookie logs. Serve immediately, or store in an airtight container, refrigerated, up to 1 week.

swedish ginger cookies

MAKES 3 DOZEN

- ¾ cup strained bacon fat
- 1 cup sugar, plus more for rolling
- 4 tablespoons dark molasses
- 1 large egg
- 2 cups all-purpose flour
- ¾ teaspoon salt
- 2 teaspoons baking soda
- 1 teaspoon ground ginger
- 1 teaspoon ground cloves
- 1 teaspoon cinnamon

1. Preheat the oven to 350°F. In the bowl of an electric mixer fitted with the paddle attachment, cream bacon fat and sugar. Beat in molasses and egg. Add the remaining ingredients; combine thoroughly.
2. Shape dough into walnut-sized balls, roll balls in sugar, and flatten with fingers on ungreased baking sheets. Bake until cookies are golden brown and cracked on tip, 10 to 12 minutes. Transfer to wire racks to cool. Store in an airtight container, up to 1 week.

lemon cream cheese bows

MAKES ABOUT 5 DOZEN

We baked these cookies in a bow shape, but they could also be piped into wreaths, numbers, or letters of the alphabet.

- 1 cup (2 sticks) unsalted butter
- 1 3-ounce package cream cheese
- 1 cup sugar
- 1 large egg
- 1 teaspoon finely chopped lemon zest
- 2 tablespoons freshly squeezed lemon juice
- 3 cups sifted all-purpose flour
- 1 teaspoon baking powder
- Confectioner's sugar, for sprinkling

1. In the bowl of an electric mixer fitted with the paddle attachment, cream butter and cream cheese. Beat in sugar. Add egg, lemon zest, and lemon juice; mix well. Sift together flour and baking powder; work into butter mixture.
2. Transfer dough to the refrigerator to chill for several hours.
3. Preheat the oven to 375°F. Using a pastry bag with a star tip, pipe dough into bows or desired shapes. Bake for 8 to 10 minutes. Transfer to wire racks to cool and sprinkle with confectioners' sugar.

peach-oatmeal cookies, page 6

fruit jumbles, page 13, and peanut butter no-bakes, page 24

swedish ginger cookies, page 25

butter cream cookies with chocolate glaze, page 14

big ginger cookies, page 4

lemon cream cheese bows, page 25

rugalach, page 41

almond lace cookies, page 23

key-lime sablés, page 16

cranberry-lemon squares, page 43

raspberry-almond crumb cookies, page 37

raspberry-almond crumb cookies

MAKES ABOUT 2 DOZEN

Pastry cutters are used as molds for these tart-like cookies; butter the pastry cutters well so they will slip off easily after baking.

- 1½ cups very finely ground blanched almonds (5¼ ounces)
- 1¾ cups all-purpose flour
- ¾ cup sugar
- ¼ teaspoon salt
- 14 tablespoons (1¾ sticks) unsalted butter, room temperature
- ½ cup plus 2 tablespoons seedless raspberry jam

1. Preheat the oven to 350°F. Line two baking sheets with parchment paper; set aside. Butter 22 two-inch fluted stainless-steel pastry cutters; place them 1 inch apart on the baking sheets. In a large bowl, whisk together almonds, flour, sugar, and salt.

2. Use a pastry blender or two knives to cut butter into dry ingredients until crumbly, then work with your fingers until there are no dry crumbs. Squeeze mixture, making pieces ranging from pea-size to 1 inch.

3. Place 2 tablespoons of crumb mixture into each pastry cutter. Press crumbs to compress into a ¼-inch thick layer.

4. Spoon 1¼ teaspoons of jam on dough; spread jam to within ⅛ inch of the edge. Sprinkle 2 tablespoons of crumb mixture over jam.

5. Bake 15 minutes, rotate sheets between oven shelves, and bake until cookies are golden brown, about 15 minutes more.

6. Transfer sheets to wire rack. Immediately lift off pastry rings; let cookies cool completely. Store in an airtight container.

chocolate-meringue cookies

MAKES ABOUT 3 DOZEN

¼ cup plus 2 teaspoons cocoa powder
Swiss Meringue (recipe follows)

1. Preheat the oven to 175°F. Line a baking sheet with parchment paper.
2. Sift ¼ cup cocoa over the meringue, and fold so that streaks of cocoa remain.
3. Fill a pastry bag fitted with an Ateco #5 star tip; pipe cookies onto prepared baking sheet. Sift remaining 2 teaspoons cocoa over cookies; bake 2 hours, until cookies lift off parchment easily.

swiss meringue

MAKES 4 CUPS

Swiss meringue is best for piping into shapes that are to be baked until crisp. It can be rewhipped if necessary.

4 large egg whites, room temperature
1 cup sugar
Pinch cream of tartar
½ teaspoon pure vanilla extract

1. Fill a medium saucepan one quarter full with water. Set the saucepan over medium heat, and bring water to a simmer.
2. Combine egg whites, sugar, and cream of tartar in the heatproof bowl of an electric mixer, and place over saucepan. Whisk constantly until sugar is dissolved and whites are warm to the touch, 3 to 3½ minutes. Test by rubbing between your fingers.
3. Transfer bowl to electric mixer fitted with the whisk attachment. Whip, starting on low speed and gradually increasing to high, until stiff, glossy peaks form, about 10 minutes. Add vanilla, and mix until combined.

cookie-press cookies

MAKES 2 TO 3 DOZEN

For more colorful cookies, you can sprinkle them with colored sugars; here we adhere two cookies together with melted chocolate.

- 1½ cups (3 sticks) unsalted butter, plus more for sheets
- 1 cup sugar
- 2 large egg yolks
- 3¾ cups sifted all-purpose flour
- ¼ teaspoon salt
- 1 tablespoon pure vanilla extract
- 6 ounces semisweet chocolate, chopped

1. Preheat the oven to 350°F. Grease two baking sheets with butter; set aside.
2. In the bowl of an electric mixer fitted with the paddle attachment, cream butter and sugar until light and fluffy. Add egg yolks, flour, salt, and vanilla. Mix thoroughly.
3. Fill a cookie press with dough, and turn out cookies on prepared baking sheets, spaced 1 to 2 inches apart.
4. Bake until lightly browned, 10 to 15 minutes. Transfer to a wire rack to cool.
5. In a heat-proof bowl set over a pan of simmering water, melt chocolate. Spread chocolate on bottom of a cookie. Adhere a second cookie to chocolate to form a sandwich; repeat with remaining cookies. Store in an airtight container up to 1 week.

Hints From Martha:

For smaller cookies, use the #1 stop on the cookie press; use the #2 stop for larger cookies.

Don't overrefrigerate the dough; it needs to be pliable to leave the press easily. If dough appears to be too sticky to work with, try refrigerating it 10 to 15 minutes. Soft dough should be gently inserted into the barrel of the press.

blueberry pinwheels

MAKES ABOUT 3 DOZEN

Shortbread dough is cut into pinwheels for an elegant look.

- 1 cup (2 sticks) unsalted butter
- ½ cup sugar, plus more for sprinkling
- 1 tablespoon pure vanilla extract
- 1 large egg
- 2½ cups all-purpose flour, plus more for work surface
- 1 large egg yolk mixed with 1 tablespoon water, for glaze
- 1 cup good-quality apricot preserves
- Blueberries, for garnish

1. Preheat the oven to 325°F. In the bowl of an electric mixer fitted with the paddle attachment, cream butter and sugar on medium-high speed until smooth. Add vanilla and egg; mix on low speed until smooth. Stir in flour.

2. Roll out dough on a lightly floured surface to a ⅛-inch thickness and cut out 3-inch rounds. Score each round with a knife from edge almost to center 5 times, leaving ½ inch of center intact. Carefully fold down left corner of each wedge into center and press down gently, creating a pinwheel shape. Brush with egg glaze and sprinkle with sugar.

3. Bake until light brown, about 20 minutes. Transfer to wire racks to cool. Spoon preserves into center and garnish with a blueberry.

rugalach

MAKES 2 DOZEN

This recipe includes ideas for several fillings.

for the rugalach:

- 1 cup sifted all-purpose flour, plus more for work surface
- ½ teaspoon coarse salt
- 8 tablespoons (1 stick) unsalted butter, chilled and cut into pieces
- 4 ounces cream cheese
- 2 tablespoons buttermilk, chilled
- ¼ cup apricot jam
- 1 egg white, lightly beaten
- ½ cup coarsely chopped nuts, such as walnuts, hazelnuts, or almonds
- ¼ cup sanding sugar

for raisin filling:

- ¼ cup golden raisins, chopped
- ¼ cup dark raisins, chopped
- ¼ cup granulated sugar
- ½ teaspoon ground cinnamon

for dried-cherry filling:

- ½ cup dried cherries, chopped
- ¼ cup granulated sugar
- ½ teaspoon cinnamon

for dried-apricot filling:

- ½ cup dried apricots, chopped
- ¼ cup granulated sugar
- Pinch of nutmeg

for chocolate filling:

- ½ cup semisweet mini chocolate morsels

1. Place flour and salt in the jar of a food processor, and pulse until combined. Add butter, and pulse 10 times. Add cream cheese; pulse until mixture is just combined. Drizzle in buttermilk; pulse until mixture just comes together when you press it with your fingers.

2. Transfer dough to a clean work surface, and shape into a flat disk; cover with plastic, and refrigerate at least 3 hours or overnight.

3. Preheat the oven to 375°F. Line two baking sheets with parchment paper; set aside. In a small bowl, combine filling ingredients of your choice. Set filling aside.

4. Divide chilled dough into three pieces. Flatten one into a disk, and return others to refrigerator. On a lightly floured work surface, roll out disk to a ⅛-inch thickness. Cut dough into a 6 ¼-inch circle. Using a pizza cutter, divide dough in half, then into quarters, then into eighths.

5. Brush each triangle lightly with jam, then sprinkle with 1 teaspoon filling mixture, being careful not to cover the narrow ends. Starting at wider end, roll up each cookie; transfer to a baking sheet. Brush each cookie with egg white, then sprinkle with nuts and sanding sugar. Chill until firm, about 15 minutes. Repeat with remaining two-thirds of dough.

6. Bake cookies until golden brown, 15 to 20 minutes. Transfer baking sheets to a wire rack to cool completely. Store in an airtight container up to 2 days.

polish tea cookies

MAKES ABOUT 2 DOZEN

From a Kostyra family recipe. At Christmastime, we make and store a big tin full of these cookies, filling them with homemade jams just before serving.

- 8 tablespoons (1 stick) unsalted butter
- ¾ cup sugar, plus 2 tablespoons
- 1 large egg yolk, lightly beaten
- 1 teaspoon pure vanilla extract
- 1 cup sifted all-purpose flour
- 1 cup blanched almonds, finely ground
- 1 large egg white, lightly beaten
- Jam, for filling

1. In the bowl of an electric mixer fitted with the paddle attachment, cream butter and sugar. Add egg yolk and vanilla; beat well. Add flour; beat again. Transfer dough to refrigerator to chill for several hours.

2. Preheat the oven to 325°F.

3. Combine almonds with two tablespoons sugar. Form dough into small balls and dip in beaten egg white, then in almond-sugar mixture. Press center of each ball with your thumb to make an indention.

4. Bake for 5 minutes, then remove and push down centers again. Bake about 15 minutes more, or until golden brown. Transfer to wire racks to cool slightly; and fill centers with jam.

cranberry-lemon squares

MAKES ABOUT 1 ½ DOZEN

These tart bars use dried cranberries instead of fresh, so you can make them any time of year.

- 6 tablespoons chilled unsalted butter, cut into 12 pieces, plus more for pan
- 1½ cups dried cranberries (about 7 ounces; available at specialty-food stores)
- 2 cups water
- ¼ cup confectioners' sugar, plus more for dusting
- 1 cup all-purpose flour
- 2 large eggs
- ¾ cup granulated sugar
- ¼ cup plus 1½ teaspoons freshly squeezed lemon juice (about 3 lemons)

1. Preheat the oven to 325°F. Butter an 8-inch square baking pan, and set aside.
2. In a medium saucepan, combine cranberries and the water; bring to a boil. Reduce heat to medium, and cook, stirring occasionally, until water has been absorbed, about 25 minutes.
3. Transfer cranberry mixture to the jar of a food processor; chop coarsely. Transfer to a bowl, and set aside.
4. In the bowl of an electric mixer fitted with the paddle attachment, combine confectioners' sugar and ¾ cup flour. Add the butter, beating on low speed until mixture forms pea-size pieces. Press batter into baking pan.
5. Bake until golden, about 20 minutes. Transfer to a wire rack to cool.
6. Beat eggs and granulated sugar until smooth. Add lemon juice; beat to combine. Add remaining ¼ cup flour, and beat to combine; set lemon mixture aside.
7. Reduce oven temperature to 300°F. Spread cranberry mixture over cooked crust. Pour lemon mixture over cranberry mixture. Bake until set, about 40 minutes. Transfer to a wire rack to cool, about 40 minutes. Chill 4 hours. To serve, cut into squares and dust with confectioners' sugar.

fruit crumb bars

MAKES ABOUT 5 DOZEN

It takes much less time to make the cranberry version of these, as there is no peeling or slicing involved.

- 2¼ cups all-purpose flour
- 1 teaspoon baking soda
- ¾ teaspoon salt
- 1¼ teaspoons ground cinnamon
- 4 cups quick-cooking oats
- 1½ cups packed light-brown sugar
- 1½ cups (3 sticks) unsalted butter, cut into ½-inch pieces
- Apple or Cranberry Filling (recipes follow)

1. Preheat the oven to 375°F. In a large bowl, whisk together flour, baking soda, salt, and cinnamon. Stir in oats and brown sugar. Using fingers, cut butter into mixture until combined; mixture should be crumbly but hold together.

2. Line an 11-by-17-inch baking pan with parchment paper. Press 5 cups oat mixture into bottom of pan. Spread filling over oat mixture. Sprinkle remaining oat mixture over filling. Bake until golden, about 40 minutes. Transfer to a wire rack to cool. Cut into about 60 1¼-by-2½-inch pieces.

apple filling

MAKES 5 CUPS

- 4 tablespoons unsalted butter
- ¼ cup plus 2 tablespoons packed light-brown sugar
- 10 Granny Smith apples, cored, peeled, and cut into ½-inch pieces
- 1 tablespoon cinnamon
- Juice of half a lemon

1. Heat 2 tablespoons butter and 3 tablespoons brown sugar in a large skillet over high heat. When butter is melted and bubbling, add half the apples. Sprinkle the apples with 1½ teaspoons cinnamon. Cook, stirring occasionally, until apples are soft and slightly golden, about 12 to 15 minutes. Transfer to a large bowl.

2. Repeat with remaining butter, sugar, apples, and cinnamon. Transfer cooked apples to a large bowl. Stir in lemon juice. Cool completely before using for cookies.

cranberry filling

MAKES 3 ¾ CUPS

If fresh cranberries are not available, frozen will work just as well.

- 6 cups cranberries
- 1 cup sugar
- ¼ cup water
- 1 cup golden raisins

Place cranberries, sugar, and the water in a medium saucepan over medium heat. Bring to a simmer, and cook until cranberries burst and the liquid they have released has become slightly thickened, 12 to 15 minutes. Stir in raisins. Transfer to a large bowl to cool completely before using for cookies.

shaker lemon bars

MAKES ABOUT 5 DOZEN

Complete step one the day before you plan to bake these cookies.

- 2 lemons, washed and dried
- 2¾ cups sugar
- 2¼ sticks chilled, unsalted butter, cut into ½-inch pieces
- ½ teaspoon salt
- 3 cups all-purpose flour
- 4 large eggs, lightly beaten
- Confectioners' sugar, for sifting

1. Slice lemons as thinly as possible; remove seeds. Toss slices with 2 cups sugar; transfer mixture to a flat resealable plastic container. Place in the refrigerator overnight.

2. Place butter, salt, remaining ¾ cup sugar, and flour in the jar of a food processor. Process until mixture is in crumbs and starts to hold together.

3. Preheat the oven to 400°F. Line an 11-by-17-inch baking sheet with parchment paper. Press dough evenly into the bottom and up the sides of the pan, making sure there are no holes. There should be at least ½-inch crust of dough going up the sides of the pan. Bake until golden brown, about 20 minutes. Transfer to a wire rack to cool completely, about 15 minutes.

4. Place lemon-sugar mixture and eggs in the bowl of a food processor. Process until lemon rinds are in ¼- to ½-inch pieces, 30 to 40 seconds. Pour mixture over cookie crust. Bake until set, 15 to 20 minutes. Transfer to a wire rack to cool. Trim ½-inch around edges of pan. Cut into about 60 1¼-by-2-inch pieces. Sift confectioners' sugar over cookies.

kathleen's lemon bars

MAKES ABOUT 3 DOZEN

This is a particularly tangy version of an old favorite.

for cookies:

- 3/4 cup (1 1/2 sticks) unsalted butter, softened
- 1 1/2 cups sifted all-purpose flour
- 1/3 cup sugar

for topping:

- 4 large eggs
- 5 tablespoons all-purpose flour
- 2 cups sugar
- 3/4 cup freshly squeezed lemon juice

1. Preheat the oven to 350°F. Combine butter, flour, and sugar. Press mixture into an unbuttered 9-by-13-inch baking pan. Bake until just turning brown, about 20 minutes.

2. For topping, lightly whisk eggs. Sift together flour and sugar; add to eggs. Add lemon juice, stir, and pour over partially baked base.

3. Bake for 20 minutes more, or until topping is firm. Chill before cutting into bars.

chocolate-fudge presents

MAKES ABOUT 3 DOZEN

Little pieces of satin ribbon transform these squares of fudge into the tiniest of gifts.

- 2 tablespoons unsalted butter, plus more for pan
- 3 tablespoons best-quality cocoa powder
- 2 cups sugar
- ⅔ cup milk
- 3 ounces best-quality semisweet chocolate, finely chopped
- 2 tablespoons light corn syrup
- 1 cup walnut halves, cut into large pieces

1. Butter an 8-by-8-by-2-inch pan. In a medium bowl, sift together the cocoa powder and sugar.

2. Prepare an ice bath. In a small saucepan, combine milk and cocoa-powder mixture with a wooden spoon until a sandy, paste-like texture forms. Add chocolate, butter, and corn syrup. Cook on low heat, stirring constantly, until sugar has completely dissolved, 7 to 10 minutes.

3. Using a pastry brush, wash down sides of pan with cold water. Increase heat to medium. When a candy thermometer registers 238°F (soft-ball stage), remove pan from heat, and place in ice bath for 5 seconds. Transfer pan to a heat-proof surface, and let sit until thermometer registers 121°F, about 45 minutes.

4. Using a wooden spoon, stir fudge briskly until it begins to lose its sheen, 2 to 3 minutes. Stir in walnuts. Spread fudge into prepared pan with wooden spoon. Using your fingers, smooth fudge. Cover with plastic; chill 30 minutes. Cut into 1-inch squares.

index

dropped

rolled

molded

bars